Learn 'n' Enjoy

VEGETABLES

AF730033

Discovery Kidz

Published By
DISCOVERY PUBLISHING HOUSE PVT. LTD.

**4383/4 - A, ANSARI ROAD, DARYA GANJ,
NEW DELHI - 110002 (INDIA)
TEL : +91-11-23279245 / 43596064 / 43596065
FAX : +91-11-23253475
E-MAIL : parul.wasan@gmail.com
info@discoverykidz.in
WEB :- www.discoverykidz.in**

TOMATO

CAULIFLOWER

POTATO

SWEET POTATO

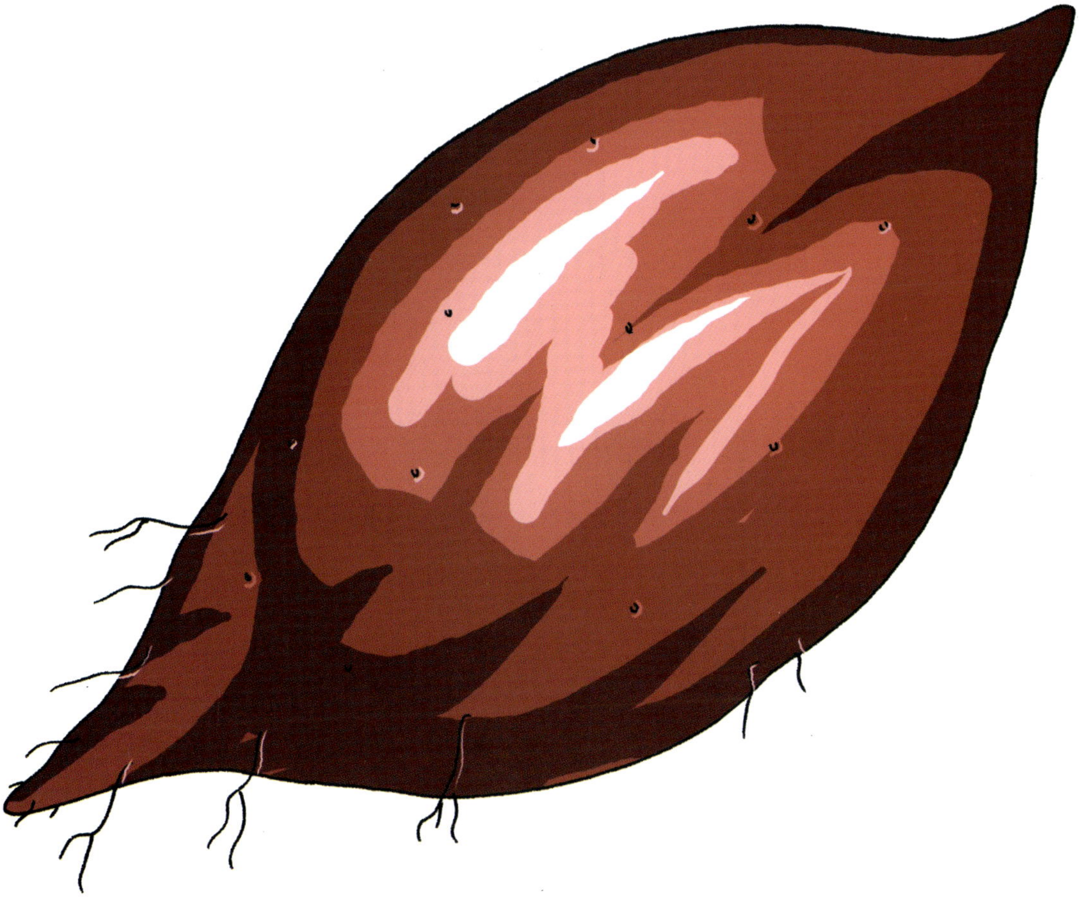

FRENCH BEANS

GREEN PEPPER

PUMPKIN

CABBAGE

EGGPLANT

SPINACH

CUCUMBER

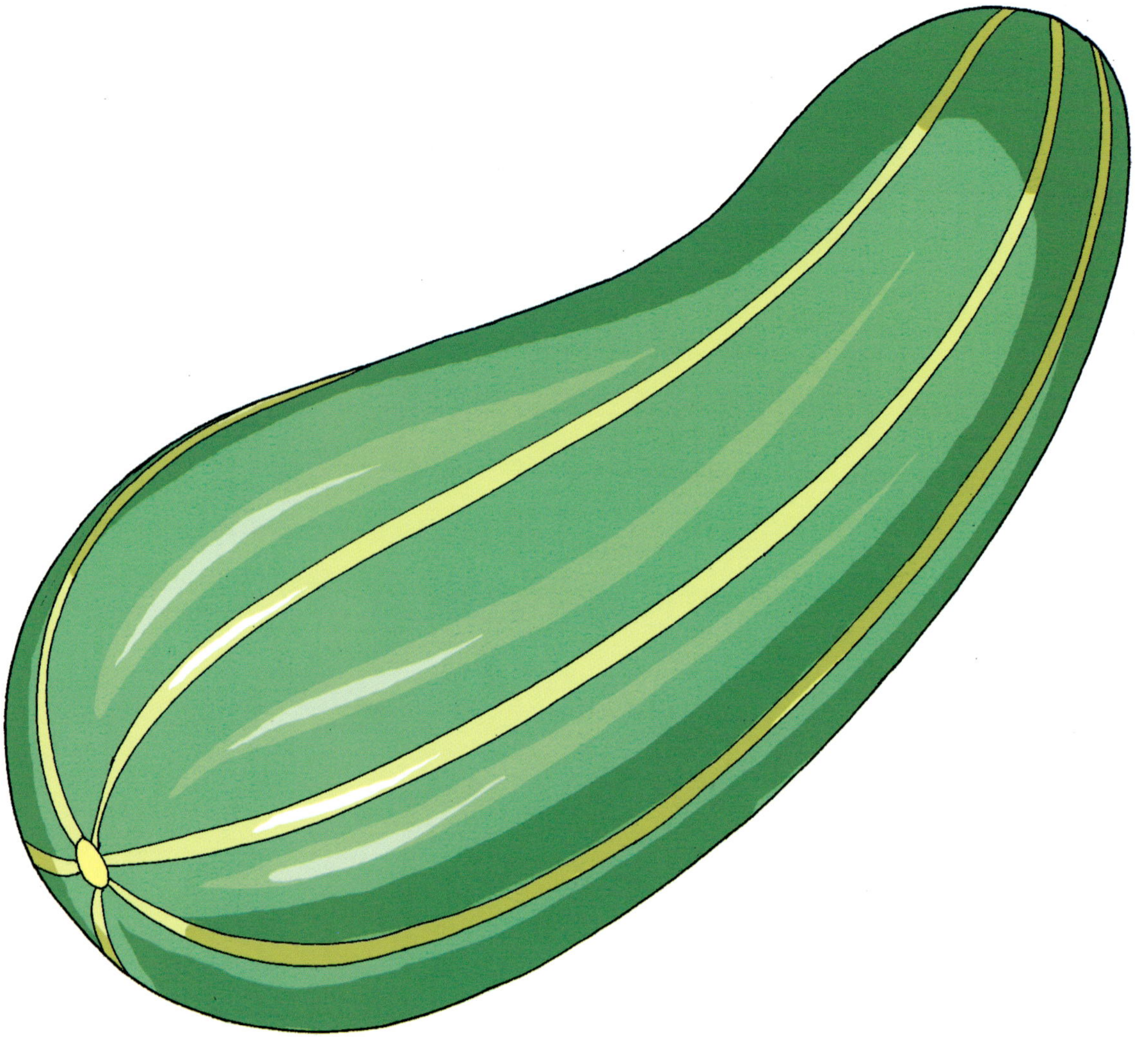

CARROT

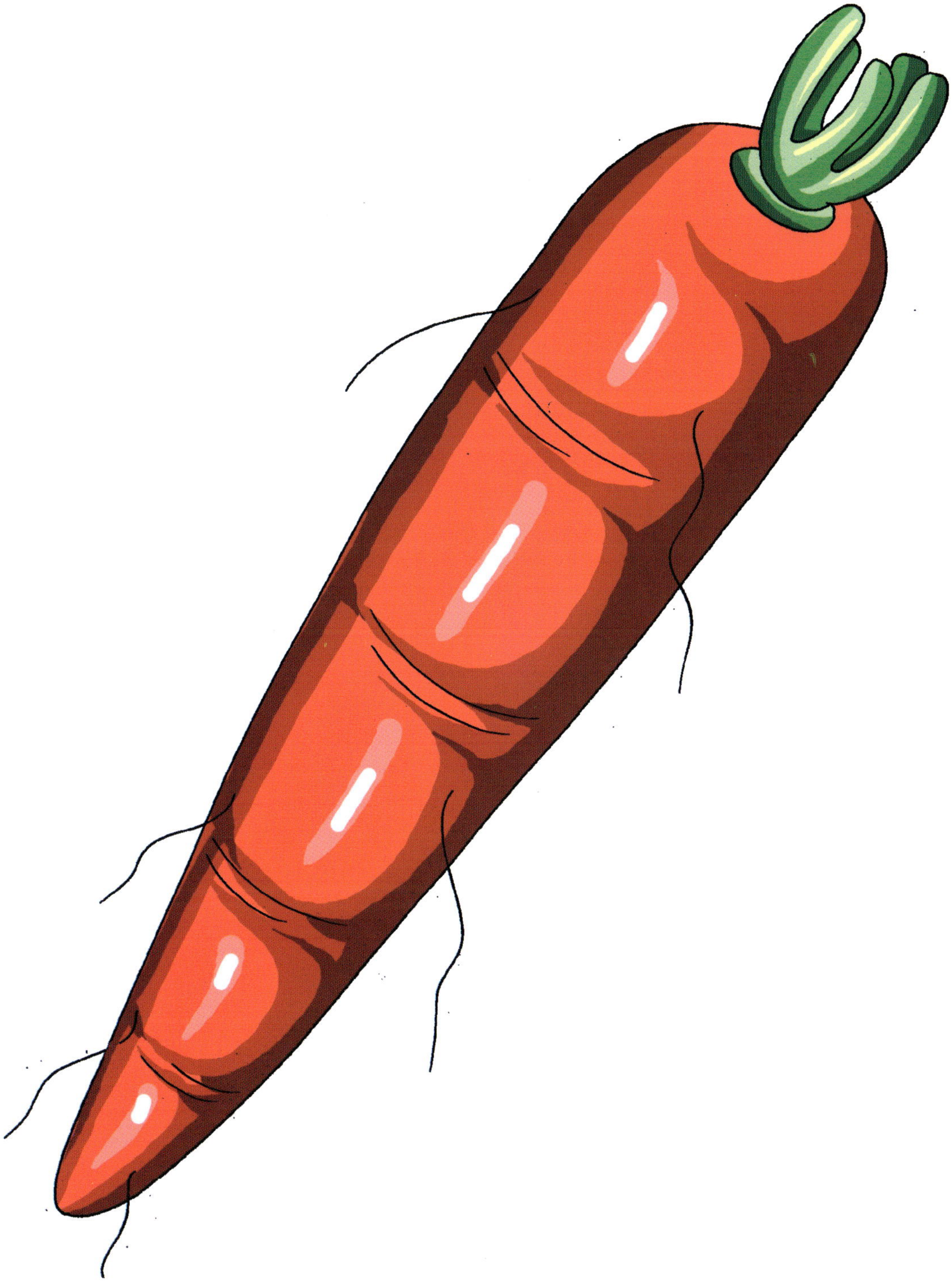

LADY'S FINGER

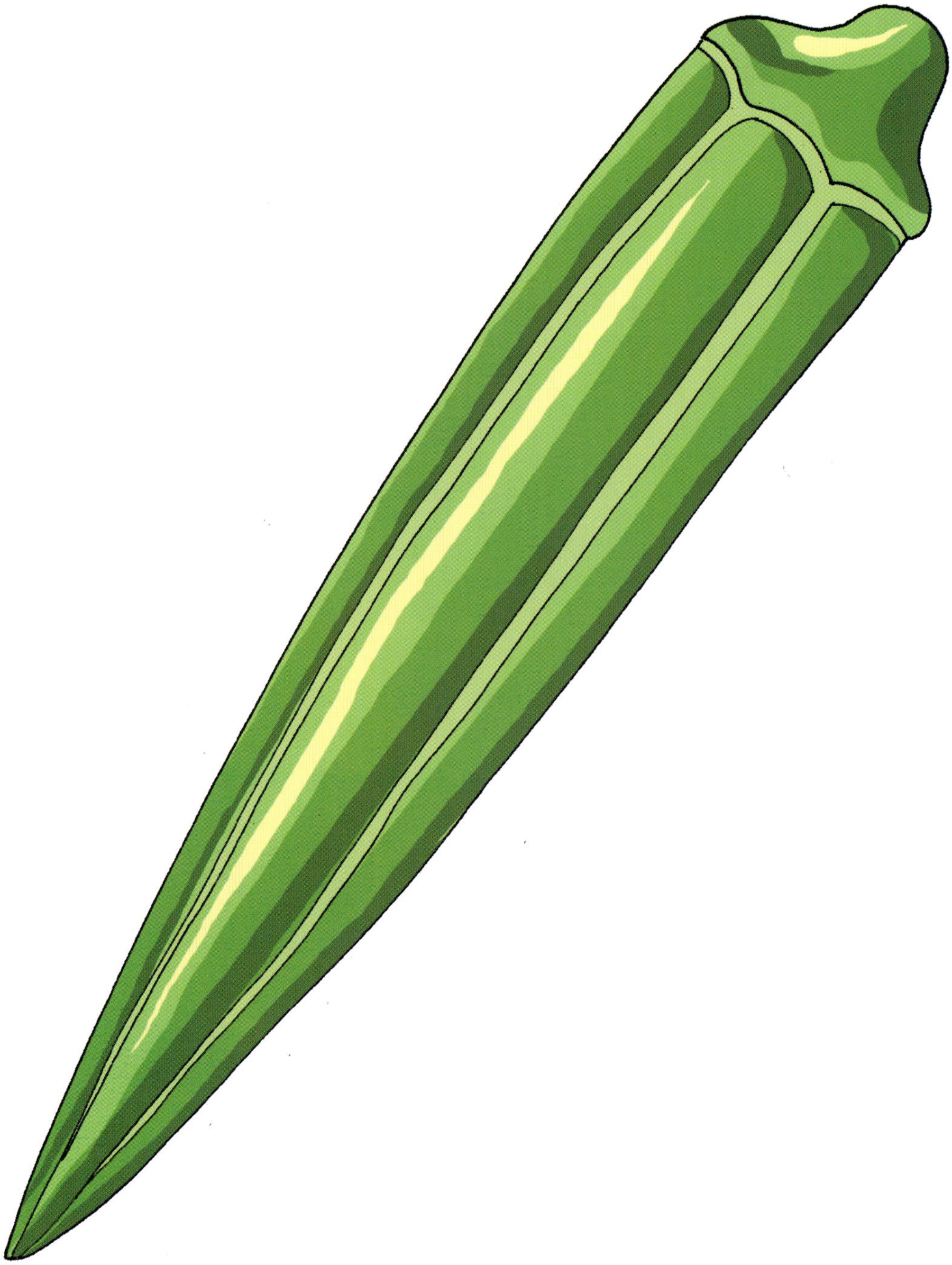

ONION

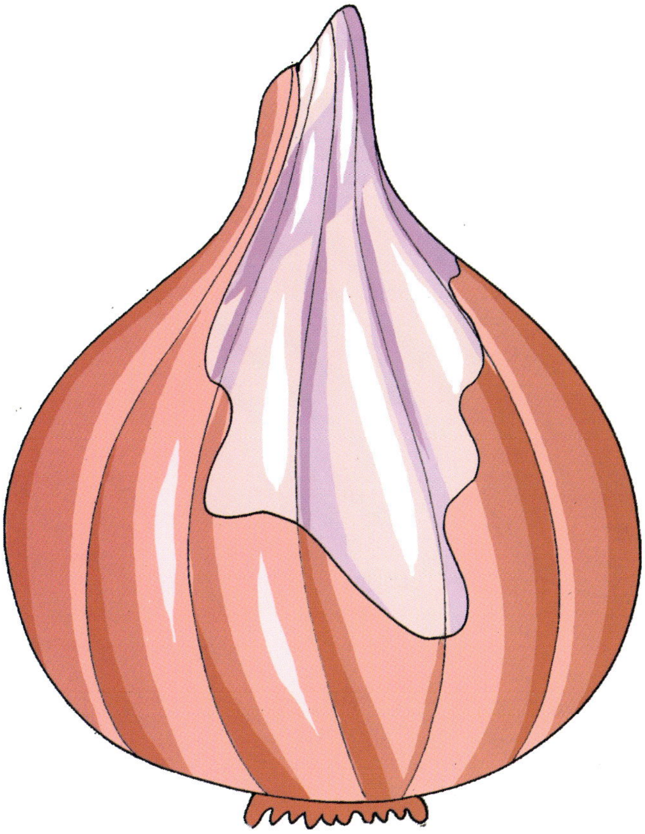

CORIANDER LEAVES

GINGER

CHILLI

GARLIC